MW01629087

EGGLESS POSSIBILITIES

By
Bat-El Gershowitz

batelskitchen@gmail.com
info@batelskitchen.com

MEDICAL DISCLAIMER

This book is NOT a medical advisory by any way , shape or form. Eggless Possibilities is intended to give you a general educational understanding and does not provide professional medical advice for any medical condition. The content and information provided is entirely derived from personal experience and therefore should not be relied on as medical or personal advice to anyone.

If you have any questions or concerns please ask for more guidance and information from your doctor or other qualified health professional.

If you think you may have any allergic reaction or medical emergency, call your doctor immediately, go to the nearest hospital emergency department, or call the emergency services immediately. By not taking any of these actions you are responsible for the consequences at your own risk. The content in this book is not a substitute for a professional diagnosis or treatment.

© copyright 2019 by Bat-El Gershowitz
First Edition
ALL RIGHTS RESERVED
This book CANNOT be reproduced, copied (physically or electronically), photographed, for Personal or Public Group , or shared via social media without a direct personal written permission from the author / copyright holder.
ISBN: 978-0-578-22880-8
Photography © 2019 by Bat-El Gershowitz

TABLE OF

Contents

Introduction

As in every new beginning, transitioning to a wholesome vegan diet can be very challenging. This was especially true for me when it came to binding ingredients together. I very much remember those times when I was overly excited to make a vegan burger or patty and things did not exactly go as planned! The texture was either too mushy or too brittle, the patties either fell apart or felt like a ton of bricks! And might I add, they looked SO unappetizing! Some recipes were so time consuming that even my famed patience waxed thin. Another realization that struck me: Not using eggs is HARD! Suddenly I sympathized with all the would-be "veganists" who gave up trying. As for the others who have gone Vegan, I suspected this was the reason they prefer to buy manufactured frozen vegan food (although it is often highly processed), or simply stay at the vegetarian stage, they did not want to face the struggle and disappointment of failing again and again.... as I did.

HOWEVER, as someone who is known to love her kitchen - including all the cooking challenges this room entails – I knew that waving my hands in despair and giving up were not options for me. What I was missing was a creative way to perfectly bind any food - without adding unhealthy ingredients that would defeat my purpose in transitioning to a vegan diet. So I kept on experimenting, checking out new and old common "binding methods", discovering new ingredients, new textures, and flavors, and; eventually my endeavors paid off. I learned the best binding techniques and how to master the blueprint of plant-based food. I'm beyond blessed to be able to put all of my discoveries down in print and to share them with my fellow interested companions to lead a vegan lifestyle.

This book is unique in that it is not a portfolio of hundreds of recipes. Instead, I ask you to look at it as a basic training manual. It is totally about teaching the techniques of what you can do with simple and extremely healthy ingredients! One of these (I like to call it "the star of the show" as it was the nucleus for creating this book) will appear in 90% of the recipes. After working with it and getting to "know" its texture and how it can improve any dish, I took it to the next level. The result was different flavors, varied combinations, and a whole new set of delicious dishes to serve my family. I invite you too, to let loose and enjoy putting the fun back in cooking.

Since this book is a total game changer, I consider it a must-have for every new or experienced vegan and would-be vegan. This book is also life changing for those forced because of medical conditions to abstain from eggs, dairy, nuts or flour. Almost all of these recipes are free from gluten, soy and nuts.

As you read through my book, you will see that the majority of the dishes are patties, burgers, or meatballs, all of which freeze beautifully in ziplock bags. If by any chance you have leftovers (I highly doubt it!), put them in the fridge. They will taste just as good on the following day, and you will gain an amazing lunch. Add them to your breakfast sandwich, place them in your salad, or just dip them into your favorite tahini sauce. The options are endless. (Or should I say eggless!)

Although most of the recipes in this book are oven friendly, I encourage you to first try pan-searing in a NON-STICK pan (unless the recipe specifies that the best method is baking). The amount of oil used in searing is extremely low; and if you use an oil spray you will use even less. Let your creative juices flow! Try searing part of the recipe and baking the rest. See what works best for you.

I highly recommend that before cooking the whole batch, always do a taste test. Check the seasonings, adjust to your palate and your family's, and then continue.

Please follow directions carefully so that you will not face situations like I did when starting out - food sticking to the pan, food not thoroughly cooked, or a dish that goes up in flames and NOT because it was flambeed!

Impress your family and friends by bringing a tray of these vegan delights on your next visit or occasion and leave them speechless when you reveal that not one single egg or bread crumb was used to bind in the making any of these dishes.

Enjoy living a healthy lifestyle, and never give up trying to eat healthy. Ignore the negative comments of people who say, "You only live once, enjoy the junk food while you can". Tell them that having only one life to live is PRECISELY the reason you want to eat healthy and be able to enjoy nature's bountiful essences. Encourage them to try making your favorite recipes. Who knows? They may become passionate vegans!

I would love to hear from you. Please share your experiences with me via the email address printed below. Remember - becoming a vegan is a challenge, but this book is going to change your life for the better. And if I was able to do it, I'm sure that you can too.

Stay tuned for my online cooking demo classes on how to cook the highlights of this cookbook.

With love and blessings for your success,

Bat-El

info@batelskitche.com
batelskitchen@gmail.com

Thank You!

This book is dedicated to

To G-d: For blessing me with a passion for food and a healthy lifestyle. For giving me the talent to create healthy masterpieces that rejuvenate both body and soul. For allowing me to empower other moms, families and children to live a healthy life in a healthy body. For putting me through my own journey of understanding until I finally comprehended the meaning of healthy food. Today, because of You, I have taken that understanding one step further and through my book will show the world how easily we can enjoy the abundant gifts of nature.

To Eli, my beloved husband: For encircling me with endless support so that I can live my passion and accomplish my dreams. Thank you for being there for me, for always being so understanding, and for travelling with me hand in hand on this incredible journey! You planted the seeds for this project and now we are both reaping the fruits of my endeavors.

To My children: You are my beginning, my center, and my essence. Thank you for allowing me the utter bliss of motherhood.

To Mom and Dad: For being so proud of me, and for letting me know it! Thank you for all the positive encouragement towards my dreams.

To My dear Mother-in-law, Rachelle: For being my voice, for being available to put your professional twist on my writing skills, and for doing it all with a smile.

To Michal Goldshmid: My smartest friend on the planet! For being my brain, breaking your head day and night to come up with the magnificent name of this revolutionary book! I couldn't have done It without you.

To My soul friend who is more like a sister, Kelly Esther: For understanding my very dynamic imagination and for living this journey with me. You are my fuel!

To Neryk Davydov: For your wisdom, kindness and marketing input every step of the way. You are an inspiration!

To Rachel Israel: For your photography tips and for your emotional support in believing in me on this big journey.

And lastly, an enormous thank you to my beyond special health mentor, **Michal Isseroff**. You have made my transition to this healthy lifestyle a wonderfully smooth one, filled with your support and pertinent information. I could not have asked for a better messenger and mentor than you. Thanks for your unconditional love, for your genuine admiration and for sharing your vast knowledge that changed my life and so many others. May you always be blessed. I love you!

Common binding foods in the eggless world:

Chickpea flour
Flaxseeds
Chia seeds
Red lentils
Tofu
Banana
Apple sauce
Oats
Flour
Baking soda+ vinegar

I would like to share my own personal experience with some of these binders so that people who are very new to the vegan diet can have a clue of what to use and when to use it.

Chickpea flour- Great for savory dishes, gluten free, rich in fiber and protein, dominant flavor. Great for omelets, frittatas, or anything that has to do with a savory egg resemblance.

Flaxseeds- Rich in omega and fiber, great for cakes and baked goods, once combined with water the texture is very close to egg, jelly-like.

Red lentils- Once soaked in water the lentils develop its starches which allow any patties, fritters, and omelets to stick and bind. Red lentil flour is similar to chickpea flour behavior wise, however, the flavor is a bit milder.

Oats- Promotes heart health, cholesterol level, and amazing for baked goods. When replacing an egg, oats have a tendency to get dry and dance, but still work amazing when incorporated properly. Can also be gluten free.

Chia seeds- works the same as flaxseeds, chia provides a jelly like consistency and binds baked goods consistently well. Chia seeds are more dominant in color and texture unless grounded before using.

Banana- My very favorite to incorporate in sweet baked goods. A great egg replacement and a natural sweetener. Provides a moist and airy texture.
Apple sauce- also acts like banana, however, better known to replace oil in baked recipes.

Tofu- Contains soy, firms up once it comes across heat. Great for quiches, fillings, and commonly used to replace the texture of scrambles eggs.

Flour- Although low in nutrition, regular flour is always a saver. Natural in flavor and once mixed with some water it provides a sticky and thick coating to any breaded food where eggs usually do the job. I replace regular white flour with white- spelt; a much healthier grain with a variety of nutritional values.

Revealing The Secret

When we first hear the word buckwheat, the first thing that usually comes to mind is the known healthy Kasha Russian dish. Once entering the vegan path I slowly added to my kitchen more and more seeds and grains. One of them was the humble buckwheat. I had no idea that buckwheat comes in two different forms: toasted and untoasted (green- raw). Trying to cook with the common and popular toasted dark buckwheat was always a failure. It was never appetizing to me and I just couldn't adapt to the strong- dominant, somewhat overpowering smell. I knew I wanted more verity of foods other than rice, quinoa, bulgur and couscous and I kept getting exposed to new grains, seeds and plant-based products.

To those who don't know, buckwheat is a seed full of fiber, rich in magnesium and potassium, that is easy to digest, sustains energy, and helps the body detoxify from harmful aging toxins. It is an excellent food source for people with gluten intolerance and recommended for diabetics due to its low glycemic index.
Continuing with my vegan experiments and my unsuccessful binding techniques in the kitchen, one day I came across a recipe for buckwheat tortillas! It looked pretty interesting and easy to prepare. After a few trials and adjustments it became a hit in my house. (See recipe in page 127-128)

Introducing the Buckwheat Egg

The amazing legumes, grains and beans, are commonly full of healthy starches that develop once soaked in water. We're all familiar with the versatile chickpea- garbanzo beans, used commonly in the Middle Eastern falafel dish. No eggs are ever used in order to hold the mixture. Buckwheat behaves similarly. So if falafel is good without eggs, why don't we just use garbanzo beans to "veganize" and bind every food that we want?!

From all the common binders in the vegan world such as chickpea flour, red lentils, flax seeds, chia seeds and so forth... The humble raw green buckwheat is the only ingredient that is most neutral in flavor and texture. It does not overpower or overwhelms the ingredients you are trying to bind. It cooks quickly and the process is always easy and practical. How fun!

One Ingredient Eggless Possibilities

Why buckwheat? And why Raw? In no time, I fell in love with the delicate/ neutral taste of this extremely healthy grain. I simply started to buy raw (untoasted) buckwheat more and more. As part of my passion of developing recipes in my kitchen, I knew I would want to make new recipes with it, so my family and I can all benefit from the amazing nutrition value it offers. I kept testing the behavior of how this humble grain performs when working with the base of the initial tortilla recipe (of soaking it over night), but at the same time playing and replacing the recipe's ingredients, quantities and water ratios.

It came down to the point of eliminating all the water and replacing buckwheat with popular recipes that normally call for soaked red lentils. This replacement would bind the mixture instead of using eggs. Sounds confusing? I'll explain!

Eight Easy Steps To A Successful Binding Process

1. Measure

2. Place in a bowl

3. Soak overnight

4. Strain

5. Rinse

6. Place in a food processor

7. Scrape the edges

8. Process until very very smooth

A Word to the Wise
How to be prepared without panic?!

Because almost all the recipes in this book call for raw green buckwheat presoaked for at least 6-8 hours in advance (the recipes are going to be easy, I promise!), we must make sure that we have buckwheat on hand at any given time! It is our new egg replacement!

So first of all, don't be disappointed if your regular grocery store doesn't carry a product even close to looking like buckwheat. And in case that you do find it, it is most likely the common toasted buckwheat grouts (know as kasha) which would not give us the results we want.

Instead, check out your local health stores; for raw green untoasted buckwheat, purchase it online, or if you are lucky like me and happened to have a Russian grocery store nearby, you will most likely find it there for a very good price.

I also advise you to presoak the buckwheat and then store in the freezer in individual sandwich bags (see pictures). It is one of my favorite kitchen tricks of doing meal-prepping.

When needed for a recipe, I simply place the frozen batch in a colander, wash it under room temperature running water, and, it is ready to use in less than 5 minutes.

For best results, I recommend using a small food processor and a small spatula to scrape down the edges.

If you don't have 6-8 hours to soak your buckwheat, use boiling water, and soak buckwheat for 25-30 minutes. Then continue the recipe as directed. (For best results though I recommend soaking for 6-8 hours)

soaked
Soaked
Soaked
Soaked

Welcome to the Raw Buckwheat Wonders

The above food alternatives provide revolutionary binding technique that I'm beyond excited to share with the world. Vegans, their children, and even meat lovers, can all gather around the table and enjoy endlessly satisfying and healthy variety of eggless possibilities!

Baked goods Egg Substitutes Chart:

Ripe banana:

½ banana= 1 egg

Chia seeds:

1 tbsp+1/3 cup water=1 egg

Ground flax:

1 tbsp+ 3 Tbsp water= 1 egg

Apple sauce:

¼ cup=1 egg

Nut butter:

3 tbsp= 1 egg

Raw soaked and ground Buckwheat:

¾-1 cup=3 eggs

About the author

Bat-El Gershowitz is the founder of the healthy colorful blog Batel's Kitchen. She is a wife, mother, blogger, chef and health food advocate. Her passion is to educate and teach moms, parents, schools, kids and teachers about healthier food choices. Bat-El strongly believes that even the simplest food should be presented in an appetizing and extraordinary way. She's been invited to numerous events and private boutique classes to present her unique style and share from her healthy food passion, showing how simple it is to eat healthy and live a well balanced lifestyle. Bat-El was born and raised in Israel, lives in Miami, Florida with her husband and kids. She loves implementing her Moroccan background into her cooking style, using Middle- Eastern spices and flavors to enhance every dish.

Website: batelskitchen.com
Facebook: batelskitchen
Instagram: Batelgershowitz
Pinterest: Batel's Kitchen

PATTIES & BURGERS

Zucchini Patties

I find myself loving everything that's made with zucchini. This humble vegetable should be given a lot of respect due to its wonderful nutritional value. It is low carb, full of water, healthy and so versatile. These patties are made with rice which gives it such a delicious meaty flavor. I love eating them with a chopped Israeli salad or inside a sandwich.

INGREDIENTS

1 cup Buckwheat, soaked in water overnight

3 cups pre-cooked round (or brown) rice

2-3 grated zucchini

4 scallions finely chopped

½ cup chopped parsley

½ cup chopped dill

Handful cilantro

1 tbsp onion powder

1 tbsp garlic powder

Salt and pepper to taste

INSTRUCTIONS

1. Strain and rinse buckwheat very well under water. Place in a food processor and blend until very smooth. Transfer to a wide bowl.
2. Add grated zucchini, herbs, rice, onion powder, garlic powder, scallions, salt and pepper. Mix well.
3. Heat a wide non-stick pan and spray a thin layer of oil. Using an ice cream scooper, scoop the batter and place on the hot pan. Cover and let it cook on one side for 5 minutes. Flip carefully and cook on the other side until golden brown.
4. Let cool for at least 15 minutes.

Carrot + Pea Quinoa Patties

These patties not only are amazing health-wise but also totally kid friendly. Full with protein and iron, gluten-free, they are great for school lunch, and fairly easy to make. When it comes to kids, I love incorporating small peas and carrots for texture and it definitely makes it more interesting and colorful to eat. Feel free to play with the spices and add any additional seasonings that come to mind. You'll never get bored of a plain quinoa sitting in the fridge again.

Carrot + Pea Quinoa Patties

INGREDIENTS

1 cup dry raw buckwheat, soaked in water overnight

3/4 th cup dry quinoa, cooked in 1.5 cups water for 15 minutes (plain)

1 small bag frozen peas & carrots (you can add corn as well)

2 Tbsp grapeseed or olive oil

1 big onion, chopped small

Salt (about 1 tsp)

Pepper to taste

1 Tbsp onion powder

1 Tsp garlic powder

1 Tbsp nutritional yeasts (optional)

1 Tbsp fajita or Italian spice

INSTRUCTIONS

1. Place ¾ cup quinoa in a small sauce pan. Pour 1.5 cups water and bring to a boil. Cover and simmer on very low for 15 minutes. Keep the pot closed for another 5-7 minutes. (That should yield 1.5 cups of cooked quinoa)
2. While quinoa is cooking, place the oil and chopped onion in a wide skillet. Mix for a minute or two. Add the bag of peas and carrots and continue mixing until nice and soft. Season with salt and pepper, lower the heat, and cover for 10 minutes. Mix some more in between.
3. Drain and rinse the buckwheat, place in a food processor and let it blend until very very smooth (about 2 minutes). Transfer to a wide bowl.
4. Add the cooked quinoa and the sautéed peas and carrots along with the spices and fold everything together until well incorporated. Check for salt and pepper!!!
5. Heat up a big wide nonstick pan. Spray or put ½ Tbsp grapeseed oil. Then start shaping and place the patties in the pan.
6. Cook the first side for about 3-4 minutes, then flip and cook on the other side for 2-3 minutes more.
7. Place a paper towel over a plate before transferring the patties. Let them sit for 5 minutes in order to get even firmer. Then serve room temperature or warm. Enjoy!

Baked Sweet Potato Burger

I have tried so many ways to successfully achieve the right texture to my sweet potato burgers! One of the challenges were to keep it gluten free and keep it on the healthy side. Most sweet potato burgers require bread crumbs, eggs and flour to bring it to the right texture. To replace those common ingredients, we can use oats, cooked rice, and smashed garbanzo beans. This burger is a health bomb because it is not only packed with amazing protein and nutrients but it is also baked and so delicious! If you choose to give it to your kids without the bun, just form smaller patties.

Baked Sweet Potato Burger

INGREDIENTS

¾ cup buckwheat, soaked overnight

1-2 medium size sweet potatoes

2 onions, sauté

1 cup cooked garbanzo beans, mashed

1 cup quick oats (or 1 cup cooked brown rice)

1 tsp paprika

1 tbsp garlic powder

Salt and pepper to taste

½ a jar of sweet chili sauce (optional)

INSTRUCTIONS

1. Boil sweet potatoes until fork tender. Peel, mash and set aside.
2. Sauté the onions in a skillet until golden. Prepare 1 cup quick oats according to package instructions. Let cook a bit.
3. Drain, wash and grind the soaked buckwheat in a food processor until very smooth. Transfer to a bowl. In the same food processor add the garbanzo beans and pulse until crumbled.
4. In a bowl combine: Mashed sweet potatoes, ground chickpeas, onions, oats/ rice, ground buckwheat, spices. Mix well.
5. Preheat your oven to 420 F. Prepare baking sheet lined with parchment paper. Use wet hands and shape 6-8 patties-burgers. Bake for 15 minutes. Take out, brush some chili sauce on top of each burger. Place back in the oven and bake for additional 10 minutes or so. Let cook for 15 minutes to allow it to form and prepare your burger bun.

Aruk - Heavenly Iraqi Potato Patties

I have so many childhood memories eating these addictive potato patties. These are ideal to make whenever you have mashed potatoes leftovers. On the other hand, they are totally worth even making them from scratch. I love making them all year long but mainly on Hanukkah. These originally are made with eggs and flour. But thanks to the amazing powerful buckwheat, we are ok without it.

INGREDIENTS

1 cup buckwheat, soaked in water over night

4-5 medium potatoes- peeled and boiled in water until fork tender

5 green onions-finely chopped

1 cup chopped parsley

1 ½ tsp salt (or to your taste)

½ tsp ground black pepper

INSTRUCTIONS

1. Mash the potatoes with a potato masher in a bowl.
2. Add the green onions, salt, pepper, parsley and mix.
3. Drain and wash the buckwheat in a strainer and place in a food processor. Blend until very very smooth for 2 minutes. Transfer into the mashed potato bowl. Mix well and check for salt and pepper.
4. Heat up a wide nonstick pan with 1-2 tbsp oil. Using an ice-cream scooper (or wet hands), form medium- small patties; carefully drop each patty into the pan.
5. Lower the heat to medium, then cover. Sear for about 4 minutes. When the bottom side is golden brown, Flip. Let them cook for another 2-4 minutes.
6. Cool 7-10 minutes before serving!

Moroccan Style Lentil Patties

I truly love incorporating lentils in my weekly menu. But when not using eggs, lentil patties can get tricky as the texture is often too soft and mushy. This recipe changes the whole story. These hearty and filling patties are easy to shape. They also hold their shape beautifully. Perfect for lunch the next day or simply delicious when served with tahini sauce.

Baked Tofu and Spinach Mushroom Patties

Whenever I feel like we need more power leafy greens in my house I go ahead and make these delicious hearty patties. Because of the mushrooms they almost feel like meat. And this way I never throw out spinach or mushrooms that are just about to go bad. Feel free to pan sear them if you want to.

INGREDIENTS

1 cup raw green buckwheat, soaked in water over night

1 block Extra Firm tofu, drained and patted dry

2 big onions, chopped

10-12 baby Portobello Mushroom, diced

5 big handfuls baby spinach, chopped

2 tablespoons grapeseed oil

Salt and pepper to taste

1 Tbsp onion powder

INSTRUCTIONS

1. Start by chopping the onions and dicing the mushrooms.
2. Heat up a big skillet with 2 Tbsp oil, add the onions and mushrooms. Add some salt and keep stirring for about 5 minutes. Crumble the tofu with your hands and add to the pan. Cook for 3 minutes more. Add the spinach mix for 2 minutes and turn off the flame. Let cool a bit.
3. Drain the soaked buckwheat, wash under running water until clear. Add to a food processor and process until very smooth. Transfer to a bowl and combine with the mushrooms and spinach mixture. Check for salt and pepper.
4. Prepare a baking sheet lined with parchment paper. Spray a thin layer of oil. Using an ice-cream scooper, form patties and carefully place on the baking sheet. Spray some oil over the patties and bake for 20-25 minutes until firm and slightly golden.
5. Let cool for 10 minutes before serving.

Jerusalem-Style Brown Rice "Chicken" Balls/ Patties

I always tend to have leftovers of cooked brown rice in the fridge. The beauty of these patties is that they resemble the texture and flavor of chicken so much! The spice that I use here has the unique of Jerusalem. It is a combination of up to 15 Middle Eastern spices called "Ras El Hanut" that creates a unique flavor profile. It goes in almost any meat kufte or kabab in traditional Israeli homes. I highly encourage you to look on-line, purchase, and add it to your spice collection. It makes such a difference. If you would like a more chicken texture, swap half or the rice amount to a soaked TVP, known as "textured vegetable protein". If you would like to have these served in a tomato sauce, I recommend baking the balls as opposed to pan searing them. If you would like to enjoy them with a salad, I recommend shaping them as little patties so they can cook evenly.

Jerusalem-Style Brown Rice "Chicken" Balls/ Patties

INGREDIENTS

1 cup green raw buckwheat- soaked over night

2 tbsp grapeseed oil

2 onions, chopped

1 3/4th cups cooked brown rice

½ cup fresh parsley

½ cup fresh cilantro

1 tsp Salt

1 tsp Pepper

1.5 Tbsp Ras El Hanut (or grilled chicken spice)

INSTRUCTIONS

1. Place oil in a skillet to heat. Add the chopped onions and sauté until nice and soft, almost starting to brown. Add salt, pepper, 1 tbsp Ras El Hanut, and mix for 30 seconds more. Turn off heat and allow to cool a bit.
2. Strain the soaked buckwheat and wash very well under running water. Transfer to a food processor and blend very well until smooth. Transfer to a bowl, add the cooked brown rice, fresh herbs, onion mixture and mix well.
3. Keep tasting and adjusting salt and pepper and add as much as you like from the spice, Ras El Hanut.
4. If pan searing: Spray a nice coat of oil on a wide nonstick skillet.
5. Wetting your hands, begin shaping small-medium flat patties. Add each patty to the pan, searing each side around 3-4 minutes until golden brown. Transfer to a plate lined with paper towels.
6. Let cool for 5-7 minutes and serve with a fresh green salad.

For baking:
Preheat oven to 385 F.
Place patties/ balls on a baking sheet lined with an oiled parchment paper. Spray a touch more oil on top and bake at 385 for 20 minutes.

Hearty Bulgur Pizza Patties

I have always loved anything that reminds me of pizza! These patties are so so meaty! The texture is rich and deep. They are a total meal with a salad on the side! Two or three of them for brunch are beyond satisfying and filling. I found them incredibly tasty even the next day. I guess it's because all the deep flavors had a chance to marry. So if you feel like making them ahead a day or two before you serve them, feel free to do so.

Hearty Bulgur Pizza Patties

INGREDIENTS

1 cup buckwheat, soaked in water overnight

1 cup bulgur, soaked in water for 3 hours

2 tbsp grapeseed oil

2 red onions, chopped

1 cup green olives, roughly chopped

½ cup canned sliced mushrooms, drained and washed

2 fresh garlic cloves, finely chopped

1 tomato, diced

3 tbsp tomato paste

¼ cup water

1 tsp oregano

1 tsp Italian seasonings

Salt and pepper to taste

INSTRUCTIONS

1. Heat up a skillet with 1-2 tbsp oil. Add the chopped onions. Mix for 2 minutes until translucent. Add the canned mushrooms, garlic, and seasonings and mix for another 2 minutes.
2. Add the diced tomato, and keep stirring until melted. Add the tomato paste, water and sprinkle some salt and pepper. Cook for 2 minutes more and turn off the heat and let cool a bit.
3. Strain the soaked buckwheat and wash very well under running water. Transfer to a food processor and mix well until very smooth. Transfer to a bowl, add the bulgur (make sure it has no water in it).
4. Add the cooked sauce from the pan, chopped olives and mix very well. Add some more salt and pepper to your liking.
5. Spray a nice coat of oil on another wide non-stick skillet, then heat. (Using medium-low heat here since the tomato paste tends to burn).
6. Using a small bowl with cold water, wet your hands and start shaping small-medium patties. You can also use an ice-cream scooper for an even size and shape. Add to the pan and sear on each side around 4-5 minutes until golden brown. Transfer to a plate lined with paper towels.
7. Allow to cool for at least 10-15 minutes before serving.

High Protein Asian Style Baked Edamame Balls

This dish is best made with some brown rice leftovers. I love reinventing any plain food sitting in the fridge and turning it into a new satisfying meal. They are healthy, packed with plant-based protein, fun to eat and perfect for a party or Asian inspired dinner. Next time you have brown rice sitting in the fridge you will know what to do. Or you might find it totally worth it to make a new batch of brown rice.

INGREDIENTS

1 cup buckwheat, soaked overnight

3 cloves garlic, chopped

5 green onion, thinly chopped

1 tbsp freshly ground ginger

2 cups edamame, (cooked for 8 minutes)

1 ½ cups pre cooked brown rice

1/3-1/2 cup teriyaki sauce

Some crushed black pepper

INSTRUCTIONS

1. Preheat your oven to 400 F.
2. Strain the soaked buckwheat and wash very well under running water. Transfer to a food processor and mix well until very smooth. Transfer to a bowl.
3. In the same food processor, no need to wash, add the 2 cups edamame, and chop for a few seconds only, just until it is slightly crushed. We want to keep the bite and texture here. Transfer to the buckwheat bowl.
4. Add the cooked brown rice, green onion, ginger, garlic, black pepper and 1/3 cup teriyaki sauce.
5. Mix everything well, form medium size balls and place on a baking sheet lined with parchment pepper.
6. Bake for 15 minutes, take the tray out of the oven, and brush some more teriyaki sauce on each ball. Bake in the oven to caramelize, after 5-7 minutes, take out and garnish with fresh cut green onions.

Baked Moroccan Style Ground Meat kabobs/ Kuffte/ Burger/Balls

You cannot get more meatier patties than these. Look at the color! Who could even believe that these are vegan? I love the Moroccan flavors of simple ingredients like cumin, paprika, garlic, cilantro. My non vegan friends couldn't believe for a second that this is not real meat! If you are craving something that looks and feels like real meat go ahead and try these!!! Feel free to shape and size them whichever way you'd like. If you are in the mood for pasta and meat balls in a tomato sauce I recommend baking instead of pan-searing. The best way to enjoy these is with a lemony tahini sauce and a good fresh Israeli salad. This recipe makes a lot of servings so you can either cut the quantity in half or freeze the cooked ones in a zip-top bag, and pop them in the microwave whenever you are ready to eat.

Baked Moroccan Style Ground Meat kabobs/ Kuffte/ Burger/Balls

---

INGREDIENTS

1 1/4 cup buckwheat, soaked overnight

1 pack vegan ground beef (13 oz /400 grams)

15-20 baby portobello mushrooms, chopped

2 Tbsp grapeseed oil

2-3 red onions, chopped

1 raw fresh beet, grated

1 tbsp Jerusalem spice or burger spice

1 tsp turmeric

1 tsp cumin

1 tsp anise (highly recommended)

1 tbsp paprika

1 tsp salt (or more)

6 cloves garlic, grated

1 bunch fresh cilantro, chopped

INSTRUCTIONS

1. Strain the buckwheat and rinse well under running water. Place in a food processor and grind until very very smooth. Place in a wide bowl and set aside.
2. Heat up two tbsp oil in a wide nonstick skillet. Add the chopped onions and mushrooms, sauté for 5-10 minutes until the mixture golden.
3. Add the "ground beef" and cook for about 4 minutes. Add all the spices, and mix for a minute and turn off the heat.
4. Add the grated beet and add to the ground buckwheat bowl. Add the cilantro, grated garlic, and the ground beef and mushroom mixture. Incorporate everything well and adjust seasonings to your taste.
5. Heat up a clean wide nonstick skillet with 1 tbsp grapeseed oil.
6. Using a small bowl with cold water, wet your hands and start shaping burgers/ kabobs/ patties. Place in the heated pan and sear on each side about 3-4 minutes until golden brown. Transfer to a plate lined with paper towels.

For a baked version:

Preheat your oven to 400 F.

Prepare a baking sheet lined with parchment paper. Arrange patties on a baking sheet, spray a touch of oil and bake for 20 minutes until firm and slightly golden.

Best eaten with a pita, tahini sauce, and Israeli salad.

Enjoy!

Baked Mexican Black Bean Portobello Burger

Black beans play such an important role in the vegan world. They are packed with protein, fiber, and antioxidants. They have a unique rich and meaty flavor. This recipe is full of yummy flavors and spices and the texture is rich and satisfying. Feel free to shape them as big or little as you want.

INGREDIENTS

1 cup Buckwheat, soaked overnight

2 red onions, diced

2 big portobello mushrooms, diced

1 red bell pepper, diced

½ a green bell pepper, diced

1 can black beans, drained (or, 16 oz home cooked beans)

1 bunch cilantro

2 garlic cloves, chopped

2 tbsp oil

½ tbsp cayenne pepper (optional)

1 tbsp onion powder

1 tbsp fajita spice (optional)

Salt and pepper to taste

INSTRUCTIONS

1. Heat up a wide skillet with 2 tbsp oil. Add onions, peppers. Sauté for 2 minutes. Add mushrooms and garlic. Continue sautéing until nice and golden. Turn off the heat and let cool.
2. Rinse buckwheat under running water. Transfer to a food processor and blend until very smooth. Place in a wide bowl.
3. Using a fork, crush the beans until partially smashed. Transfer to the buckwheat bowl. Add mushroom and pepper mixture from the pan. Add the cilantro and spices. Mix.
4. Preheat your oven to 400 F.
5. Prepare a baking sheet lined with parchment paper. Spray a very thin layer of oil. Using wet hands form 6-8 patties and carefully place on the tray. Spray some oil and bake for 20-25 minutes until firm and slightly golden.
6. Let cool for 10 minutes. Serve with avocado, tomato, lettuce, onion, and your favorite condiments.

Baked Mexican Corn Fritters

These fritters are such a party in the mouth. Colorful, flavorful, light, healthy and pleases any kid's or adult' party and occasion.

INGREDIENTS

1 cup buckwheat, soaked overnight

1 red onion, cut in chunks

1 red bell pepper, cut in chunks

½ green pepper, cut in chunks

2 green onions, chopped

1 stalk celery, cut in chunks

1 handful of cilantro, chopped

1 can of corn, drained and divided in 2

½ a chili pepper, finely chopped (optional)

Salt and pepper to taste

INSTRUCTIONS

1. Preheat oven to 375 F.
2. Place the celery, red pepper, green pepper, red onion, and half a can of corn in a food processor. Blend until finely chopped. Transfer to a bowl.
3. Wash buckwheat under running water and place in the same food processor and blend until very smooth. Transfer to the bowl of chopped veggies. Add the rest of the corn, chopped cilantro, chopped green onions, salt and pepper and mix.
4. Prepare baking sheet lined with parchment paper. Spray a thin coat of oil. Spoon portions of the batter and press down with back of spoon. Bake for 20-25 minutes until golden. Take out and let cool for 15 minutes.

Cabbage and Carrot Veggie Burger

These patties are so so tasty! And, they are beyond healthy. This is a wonderful way to consume more cabbage in our diet which is really good for you. In this recipe, I shaped the patties big like a burger. But If you want to make it for your kids or for a big crowd go ahead and make them smaller so it will be easier to grab and hold. These patties keep beautifully in the fridge and they get even better the next day. I love eating them for breakfast, in a pita with hummus, or just on top of my salad. This quantity yields about 8 big ones or 16-20 small ones. You choose.

Cabbage and Carrot Veggie Burger

INGREDIENTS

1 cup green raw buckwheat, soaked overnight

½ a green cabbage, sliced thinly

4 carrots, grated

2 onions, chopped

2 tbsp grapeseed oil

1 tsp turmeric

1 tbsp paprika

½ tsp cumin powder

1 tsp salt (approximately)

½ tsp black pepper

INSTRUCTIONS

1. Heat up a wide nonstick skillet or pan and sautee' the onions and carrots for about 3 minutes. Add the cabbage and mix very well. Lower the heat and cook until the cabbage is soft. About 5-10 minutes. Add the spices, mix for a minute, turn off the heat and cover the pan.
2. Drain and rinse the buckwheat, place in a food processor and let it work until very very smooth for about 2 minutes. Then transfer to a wide bowl.
3. Transfer the sautéed cabbage to the buckwheat bowl and mix very well. Adjust seasonings to your taste!
4. Heat up a big, wide nonstick pan. Spray or put ½ Tbsp grapeseed oil, shape the patties and place them on the pan.
5. Cook the first side for about 3-4 minutes, then flip and cook on the other side for 2-3 minutes more.
6. Place a paper towel over a plate before transferring the patties. Let them sit for 5 minutes in order to get even firmer. Then serve room temperature or warm.

Enjoy!

Broccoli "Feta" Balls

When you need something really healthy and delicious in your menu these are totally hard to resist. Stunning on the table, kid friendly, great for a fancy party, can be eaten room temperature and just perfect overall. This broccoli mixture can also be baked as a quiche/cake/ patties or if you really want to take it to the next level, pan-sear it as a burger! It is beyond amazing!

Broccoli "Feta" Balls

INGREDIENTS

1 cup buckwheat, soaked overnight

2 big heads broccoli, cut into florets

1 pack extra firm tofu, pat dry (optional but highly recommended)

1 tbsp nutritional yeasts

2 tbsp olive oil

8 garlic cloves, minced

Salt and pepper to taste

½ cup breadcrumbs

For a quiche': place mixture on a round or 9x13 tray, sprinkle some breadcrumbs and bake for 30-35 minutes.

For a burger: Heat up non-stick pan with a thin layer of oil. Form patties and cook on each side for 3-4 minutes until golden. Let cool for 10 minutes before serving.

Enjoy!

INSTRUCTIONS

1. Bring a pot of salted water to a boil. Place the broccoli in the boiling water for 6 minutes. Take out and rinse under cold water. Place in a bowl and roughly mash with a fork. (It should be soft and falling apart with some little chucks left).
2. Pat the tofu dry and crumble into small- medium chunks.
3. Heat up 2 tbsp of oil in a wide skillet and sauté the garlic until golden brown. About 40 seconds. Add the broccoli and tofu crumbles, generously season with salt and pepper. Mix for a minute or two. Lastly, add the nutritional yeasts, stir, and allow cooling off for a few minutes.
4. Rinse and strain buckwheat. Place in a food processor and blend until very smooth. Transfer to a wide bowl.
5. Preheat your oven to 375 F. and prepare a baking sheet lined with parchment paper.
6. Combine the broccoli and ground buckwheat mixture, adjusting seasonings to raste.
7. For the breadcrumbs topping there are a few options: a). form bite-size balls and roll in to a plate with breadcrumbs; or b) place the broccoli balls on the baking sheet and sprinkle breadcrumbs on top; or c) leave it plain without any breadcrumbs at all.
8. Whichever way you choose, once placed on the baking sheet, spray a touch of oil and bake for 20 minutes.
9. Let cool and serve room temperature.

Baked Cauliflower and Red Lentil Patties

These baked patties are so yummy and healthy. I love everything that has to do with cauliflower and by adding the red lentils we get a chance to enjoy a high quality of plant-based protein. This is also a great finger food for kids! When my kids were toddlers I used to put these patties on the highchair table and let them discover textures and flavors. Add them to your sandwich, top it on your salad or snack on it at work. Whatever works for you.

Baked Cauliflower and Red Lentil Patties

INGREDIENTS

1 cup raw buckwheat, soaked in water over night

1-2 tbsp oil

2 onions, chopped

1 head cauliflower, cut into florets

¼ cup red lentils

2 carrots, grated

Salt and pepper to taste

¼ cup oat flour or breadcrumbs

1 tsp salt

¼ tsp pepper

INSTRUCTIONS

1. Bring a big pot of water to a boil. Add a little salt and cook the red lentils for 15 minutes. Add the cauliflower florets and cook for 6 minutes more until nice and soft. Drain well and let cool.
2. While veggies are cooking sauté 2 onions in 1 tbsp oil. Add the carrot and sprinkle some salt. Turn off the heat once golden.
3. Drain and rinse the buckwheat under running water. Place in a food processor and grind until very very smooth. Transfer to a bowl.
4. Preheat your oven to 400 F.
5. Place the drained cauliflower in a food processor and pulse 2-3 times until crumbly. (Best to do in 2-3 batches).
6. To the buckwheat bowl, add the sautéed onions, cauliflower and lentils, breadcrumbs, salt and pepper. Mix very well.
7. Prepare a baking sheet lined with parchment paper. Using wet hands form medium size patties and place on the baking sheet. Spray some oil on top and bake for 20 minutes or until golden. Take out, let cool for 10-15 minutes before serving.

The Ultimate Veggie Burger

This recipe is such a big hit in my house. I've always loved store bought veggie burgers but the texture was never amazing. Either they were too soft, breaking apart, or simply loaded with oil. But no more! This healthy burger is going to please any child to love their veggies.

INGREDIENTS

1 cup green buckwheat, soaked overnight

3 cups frozen veggies (peas, carrot, corn, green beans)

1 big onion, chopped

1 garlic clove, minced

2 small potatoes, cooked

1 tsp paprika

1/2 tsp turmeric

3 tbsp fresh parsley, dill, cilantro

INSTRUCTIONS

1. Bring water to a boil, place the frozen vegetables along with the potatoes and cook until the potatoes are fork tender. Drain the water, separate the potatoes, peel and mash well. Set aside.
2. In a big wide skillet sauté chopped onion until golden, add the drained vegetables along with the garlic and spices. Mix well and lower the heat. Cook for about 5-7 minutes.
3. Drain and wash the soaked buckwheat, place in a food processor and run until very very smooth. Transfer to a bowl.
4. Combine the sautéed vegetables, mashed potatoes, parsley, add some more seasonings (salt, pepper, paprika).
5. Heat up a wide nonstick skillet and spray with some oil. Wet your hands and form patties to the size that you want. Cook for 4 minutes on the first side. Flip patties and cook until golden brown on the other side. You might need to add some oil on each subsequent set of patties.
6. Take out, place on a plate lined with paper towels and let cool for 10 minutes. Serve with some Israeli salad on the side.

Baked Moroccan Fish Balls

Growing up in a Moroccan home we always had fish. Until today, my dear mother makes the best Moroccan fish balls in the world. But how do we revive this nostalgia and bring it to life in this vegan world? This recipe is very unique and satisfying since it mimics the real dish so much in both in texture and flavor!

Baked Moroccan Fish Balls

INGREDIENTS

For the balls:

1 cup raw buckwheat, soaked overnight

1 extra firm tofu, pat dry

1/2 cup chickpea flour

1 tbsp matzo meal (optional)

1 potato, peeled and finely grated (optional)

3 garlic cloves, minced

2 tbsp olive oil

1 big handful cilantro, chopped

¼ cup fresh dill, chopped

1 tsp salt (to your taste)

¼ tsp black pepper

½ tsp cumin

For the sauce:

3 tbsp light olive or grapeseed oil

1 big red bell pepper-cut in chunks

2 big fresh juicy tomatoes- cut in chunks

1/2 jalapeño or Serrano pepper, seeded and sliced

5 big garlic cloves, peeled

Big cilantro bunch- washed, dried and chopped

2 Tbsp paprika

½ tsp turmeric

1 tsp ground pink Himalayan salt (to taste)

½ tsp black pepper

¼ cup water

INSTRUCTIONS

1. Preheat your oven to 350 F.
2. Drain and rinse the buckwheat under running water. Place in a food processor and grind until very very smooth. Transfer to a bowl.
3. Squeeze out any access water from the tofu and place in a food processor. Blend until smooth and transfer to the processed buckwheat bowl.
4. Add the chickpea flour, matzah meal, grated potato, spices, garlic, cilantro, chopped dill and mix very well.
5. Prepare a baking sheet lined with parchment paper. Using wet hands, start forming medium size balls and transfer to the tray. Spray a touch of oil on top and bake for 10 minutes. Take out and let cool.
6. Prepare the sauce:
7. Place all the ingredients except the cilantro and jalapeno, in a food processor and blend until very smooth. (Tomatoes, olive oil, garlic, red bell pepper, water and spices). Once blended adjust salt and spices and pour all over the baked fish-balls, generously sprinkle the chopped cilantro and sliced jalapeno. Cover with parchment paper, then foil on top, close very well and bake for 35-45 minutes. If the sauce is too thick add a drop of water, shake the pan and serve with challah or a good piece of bread.

Enjoy

Chickpea Burger

Living a vegan lifestyle requires some extra preparation when it comes to the consumption of plant-based protein. That is why chickpeas are always found in my freezer! They are a huge part of our household diet. I buy them in a bulk, keep them in my freezer and once every two weeks or so, I soak and cook them to my desired doneness. This way I can make what I want at any given time. I make burgers, hummus, soups, and stews. Or just simply enjoy them with some salt and olive oil. This burger is a little different from the regular "falafel" flavor we are all familiar with. You can make the patties as big or little as you like.

Chickpea Burger

INGREDIENTS

1 cup green buckwheat, soaked in water overnight

2 cans chickpeas, drained and rinsed (or home cooked)

5 garlic cloves, minced

2 big onions- chopped

2 big handfuls of fresh cilantro

1/4 jalapeno pepper, chopped (optional)

1-2 tsp ground cumin

1-2 tsp salt

¼ tsp pepper

1 tsp paprika

½ tsp turmeric

2 tbsp oil

INSTRUCTIONS

1. Heat a skillet with 2 Tbsp oil. Add the chopped onions and sauté until translucent. While onions are cooking, place the chickpeas in a food processor and pulse a few times until you get a crumbly consistency. (You may use a potato masher or a fork as well).
2. Add the garlic and jalapeno pepper to the skillet and mix constantly so that the garlic doesn't burn. Add the crumbled chickpeas along with the spices, mix for a few minutes and turn off the heat.
3. Rinse and strain buckwheat. Place in a food processor and blend until very smooth. Transfer to a wide bowl.
4. Add the chickpea mixture and the chopped cilantro. Mix well until all incorporated and adjust seasonings.
5. Heat up a nonstick skillet with 2 tbsp oil. Form burgers to your desired size. Cook the first side for about 4 minutes. Flip and cook the other side until golden.
6. Remove burgers to a plate lined with paper towels. Let cool for at least 10 minutes.

For your burger:
Tahini sauce
Tomato
Lettuce
Israeli pickles
Fresh cilantro

Lemony "Crab" Cakes

Growing up in a Jewish Kosher kitchen, I have never ever eaten any crab in my life. But I knew I wanted to make this signature dish and include it in this book as it such a decadent food for so many Americans who try to enjoy it in the vegan version. I'm just speechless on how powerful nature is by providing us fruits and vegetables that totally replaces the texture and even flavor of animal products. For the crab, we are going to use hearts of palms. This recipe is really easy and so refreshing. From some reason the flavor and texture are even better the following day. So leftovers are absolutely welcomed.

Lemony "Crab" Cakes

NGREDIENTS

cup raw green buckwheat, soaked over

ıight

½ cups hearts of palm, chopped

-2 tbsp hearts of palm liquid from the jar

tbsp capers, finely chopped

red bell pepper, finely diced

red onion, very finely chopped

lemon, zested (Don't skip this one)

tbsp fresh herb of your choice, cilantro, dill,

ɔarsley

½ lemon squeezed

Salt and pepper to taste

cup breadcrumbs for coating (gf if needed)

tbsp oil

Lemony Aioli

tbsp vegan mayo

½ lemon squeezed

½ tsp dijon mustard

-2 tsp chopped dill

¼ tsp crushed black pepper

Pinch of salt (to your taste)

INSTRUCTIONS

1. For the crab meat, take out the hearts of palm from the jar and preserve 1-2 tbsp of liquid. Chop for some rough medium- small chunks and place in a bowl. (We want to have a nice texture and bite so the chunks should not be too small and not too big.)
2. Very finely chop the red pepper and red onion. Add to the bowl. (If you don't think you can't handle the very small chopping I recommend pulsing it in a food processor just for a few seconds).
3. Add the lemon zest, lemon juice, capers, herbs, and mix.
4. Drain and wash the soaked buckwheat, place in a food processor and run until very very smooth. (Make sure there is no water left once transferring to the food processor). Transfer to the "crab" bowl.
5. Combine all together, and generously season with salt and pepper. (If you like the spice old-bay, add a pinch of that too. Taste and correct seasonings to your liking.
6. Prepare a bowl with breadcrumbs. Heat up a nonstick pan with 1-2 tbsp oil.
7. Form medium size patties and place into the breadcrumbs bowl. Flip until nicely coated.
8. Sear each patty for 3-4 minutes on each side. Cook until golden brown. Continue this process and add tiny drops of oil if needed.
9. Let cool completely for at least 10 minutes before serving. It will help the texture to be more firm.
10. Serve with some fresh lemon and dip into the lemony aioli.
11. For the aioli: Mix all the ingredients in a bowl, and serve.

Note: If from some reason the buckwheat crab is too wet to work with, place in the fridge for a half hour to firm up, or simply add 1-2 tbsp breadcrumbs.

Red Kidney Bean Patties

Red kidney beans are an amazing source of fiber. They are hearty and filling. I try to add beans to our meals on weekly basis. These patties are so delicious on a salad or in a sandwich.

INGREDIENTS

1 cup raw green buckwheat, soaked over night

3 cups cooked red kidney beans (or from a can)

1 cup mashed potato

1 red onion, sautéed

2 tbsp tomato paste

2 Tbsp nutritional yeasts

3 tbsp chopped parsley

Salt and pepper to taste

Some oil for frying

Tools: Ice-cream scooper

INSTRUCTIONS

1. Soak a bag of red kidney beans overnight. Strain, wash, and cook the beans in a presser cooker for 15 minutes or until soft, drain and put in a bowl.
2. Strain the buckwheat and pulse with a food processor until very very smooth. Transfer to a bowl.
3. Add 1 cup mashed potato, 2 tbsp tomato paste, parsley, sautéed onion, salt and pepper and mix very well. Check for flavors!
4. Heat up 1-2 tbsp oil in a nonstick pan and prepare a bowl with some water. Dip the ice-cream scooper to the water first, then fill it up with the bean mixture and add it to the hot pan.
5. Cook for 3-4 minutes on the first side on medium low heat. Flip once and cook the other side until golden brown.

Enjoy!

CHICKPEA FLOUR

Potato and Veggie Frittata

This is one of my favorite dishes to serve when I invite friends for breakfast or brunch. Very impressive, filling, tasty, and elegant. Only a few minutes of work and you've got a beautiful main course to enjoy. I make sure to serve it hot, as soon as its ready, so the texture and flavor don't change. Perfect with a small salad on the side!

Potato and Veggie Frittata

INGREDIENTS

1 red bell pepper, diced

½ a green/orange/ yellow pepper, diced

2 red onion, chopped

2-3 potatoes, peeled and dice into small cubes

5 cherry tomatoes

1 ¼ cups chickpea flour

1 ¼ cups water

2 tbsp olive oil

Pink Himalayan salt to taste

¼ tsp turmeric

Black salt (optional)

INSTRUCTIONS

1. Bring a medium sauce pan with some salted water to a boil. Add the diced potatoes and cook for about 7-10 minutes, or until fork tender.
2. Heat olive oil over medium heat in a sauté pan. Add the onions and peppers and stir until golden. Add the tomatoes and let brown for a minute or two. Season with salt and pepper. Turn off the heat.
3. Strain the potatoes and set aside.
4. Place the chickpea flour in a large bowl. Season with salt and pepper and slowly add the water, constantly whisking until smooth. Add oil and potatoes, sautéed veggies, salt and pepper and fold until incorporated.
5. Using a CLEAN NONSTICK skillet heat up 1 tbsp oil. Pour the "egg" mixture and flatten with a spoon or spatula. Cover and lower the heat and cook for 10 minutes.
6. In order to flip, place a big plate on the skillet and carefully flip and transfer back to the skillet. Cook for a few minutes more.
7. Note: If you choose not to flip just make sure that the texture is hard and firm.

Gf High in Protein Chickpea Avocado Wraps

You can call it a crepe, wrap, taco, or a tortilla, but whichever one you choose, I'm letting you know that you are going to love me for this one! This recipe is quick, fast, and basically a shortcut from making a vegan chickpea flour base omelet. All we need is a really good small to medium, hot nonstick skillet. You can be creative with what you want to put inside. I love avocado spread or guacamole, but the sky is the limit. These wraps are best when hot, right out of the skillet. Otherwise they tend to get dry. I usually make them on Sunday mornings since I love watching my kids enjoying every bite.

INGREDIENTS

1 cup chickpea flour

1 cup water

1 tbsp olive oil

Salt and pepper to taste

Oil spray for coating the pan

INSTRUCTIONS

1. Measure 1 cup chickpea flour and place in a bowl, add salt and pepper. Mix. Slowly start adding 1 cup water while mixing with a whisk at the same time. Pour the rest of the water and mix very well along with the oil.
2. Heat a little oil in a medium- wide NONSTICK skillet.
3. Using a 1/3 measuring cup, pour the measured batter into the hot skillet. Roll the pan and spread it evenly. Cook for about 1- 2 minutes and flip. Cook for 20-30 seconds more and transfer to a plate. (This batch is enough for 4-5 wraps).
4. Spread avocado or any other spreads and enjoy while it's warm.

Egg Soufflés

Chickpea flour is so versatile and even magical in so many ways. These lovely individual chickpea soufflés are gluten free, and makes a perfect appetizer for a buffet or a party. They can be served warm or room temperature. Elegant, healthy and delicious. This batter consistency firms up really fast. So please follow the steps for best results.

Egg Soufflés

INGREDIENTS

For the toppings:

2 red onions, chopped

12-15 mushrooms, roughly chopped

8 grape tomatoes, halved

1-2 tbsp olive oil

Salt and pepper to taste

Fresh parsley to garnish

For the batter:

2 cups vegetable broth/water

1cup chickpea flour

1 cup water

1/2 tsp salt

INSTRUCTIONS

1. Step 1: In a big wide skillet sauté onions for 2-3 minutes. Working with high heat, add the mushrooms and continue cooking until golden (about 5 minutes) add the halved tomatoes, cook for 2-3 minutes more until it starts to get brown. Turn off the heat and let cool .
2. Step 2: Using mini muffin tin, oil each cavity with a spray or some oiled paper towel. Set aside.
3. Step 3: In a deep pot, bring 2 cups vegetable broth to a boil.

i. In a bowl place the chickpea flour and salt, slowly add water and whisk constantly until combined smoothly.
ii. Pour the chickpea mixture into the boiling vegetable broth and whisk immediately. Turn off the heat and continue whisking for 5 minutes until smooth and silky.
iii. combine the onion and mushroom mixture and leave a little in the pot to garnish the tops.
iv. Working fast so the batter doesn't get firm, use a wet spoon and transfer from the mixture to the oiled muffin tin.
v. garnish each top with the remaining mixture from the skillet.

4. Sprinkle some chopped parsley and place in the fridge for 40-60 minutes to allow firming completely.

5. Once firm and ready to serve, use a small sharp knife to remove the "eggs" from the muffin pan. Place on a plate and warm in the microwave for a few seconds. This can be enjoyed cold or room temperature as well.

NOTE:
If you wish not to make this cooked chickpea base as a soufflé, you can use it PLAIN as a replacement for tofu, called "Burmese".

6. Line a 9×13 baking sheet lined with parchment paper. Pour the hot chickpea mixture and flaten with a spoon. Place in the fridge for a hour. Take out, cut into big squares and use in your desired dishes.
7. Pan sear it, bread it, or stir fry it. Whatever comes to mind.

Savory Chickpea Pancakes

One of the reasons I love using chickpea flour in my kitchen is simply because you can literally have food on the plate in a matter of a few minutes! Once combined with water, this flour remains the color and consistency of a real egg. A great start for people who are still missing the real egg look in their diet. These pancakes are packed with fiber, protein and healthy carbs, perfect to start the day. I love serving them with a salad or just inside a pita with hummus and veggies. Feel free to make them small or big.

Savory Chickpea Pancakes

INGREDIENTS

1 cup chickpea flour

1 cup water (less 2 Tbsp)

2 tbsp olive oil

3 green onions, finely chopped

1.5 cups grated sweet potato

1 cup grated zucchini

½ cup fresh dill or cilantro

¼ tsp turmeric

½ tsp salt

¼ tsp pepper

Tools: Nonstick pan

INSTRUCTIONS

1. Place chickpea flour in a bowl along with the spices and mix. Add the water and oil slowly, and whisk constantly until very smooth.
2. Add the grated zucchini, sweet potato, dill/cilantro and mix.
3. Heat up a nonstick pan with ½ tbsp oil and pour 1/3-1/2 a cup into the pan. Allow to form and cook for 2-4 minutes before flipping the first side. Once golden, flip and cook for a few more minutes on the other side.
4. Allow sitting for 5-10 minutes before serving.
5. For leftovers, reheat in the microwave for 1-1.5 minutes.

BREAD

Eggless Bread

This yummy bread is shared with love straight from my mom's Israeli kitchen. The original recipe uses all purpose flour, but I like to mix in white and whole spelt for a more wholesome nutritious value. My mom never liked to use eggs in her bread dough since it makes it like a cake and less rustic. This recipe is easy and the texture is light and airy. Freezes beautifully and it's amazing for soup croutons. Best to rewarm in the oven before serving.

Eggless Bread

INGREDIENTS

1 kg all purpose flour (7-8 cups)

1.5 active dry yeasts

1/2 cup brown sugar

1/2 cup grapeseed oil

1 tbsp salt (Pink Himalayan)

3.5- 4 cups warm water

INSTRUCTIONS

1. In a mixer bowl place the: flour, dry yeast, sugar, and mix for a minute.
2. Have your measured oil and water ready and start with 2 cups first.
3. Leave the last two, for the end. You might not need the whole quantity.
4. Have your salt measured and ready as well.

Method:

A. Start your mixer on low and after one minute add the 2 cups water. Mix for about 2 minutes and slowly add the oil. At this point, all you need to do is raise the speed to medium (2-4) and let it work for about 2-3 minutes. Slowly, add some more water to the point that the dough starts to separate itself from the bowl. If you feel like the dough is too dry, add water little by little and after another minute or two add the 1 Tbsp of salt. The salt absorbs all the moisture that is left and should completely form a nice solid dough ball.

Mix for another 2-3 minutes. Let rest for 15 minutes, mix again on high for a moment or two, and transfer to a bigger bowl that was lightly oiled with a paper towel. Cover with a plastic bag and a towel on top and let rise in a warm place for one hour. Punch it once or twice in-between.

B. Prepare a few baking sheets lined with parchment paper. Dust your counter with some flour and transfer the dough from the bowl. Roll it on the counter so it's all lightly covered with flour. With a sharp knife, divide into the number of breads that you desire. I do 4-5 medium ones. Shape and place on the parchment paper. usimg a sharp knife, score some lines on each bread, dust with some more flour, cover with a clean towel or seal in a big plastic bag.

C). Let rise for at least 45 minutes.

D). Preheat your oven to 375F (I use the convection feature) for 15 minutes before you insert the first tray. Lower the heat to 350 F. Bake for 30-35 minutes until golden. Take out and let cool completely.

Note:
This recipe can be used for challah for shabbat.

So the dough doesn't dry out, cover the unshaped dough with a clean towel or closed big plastic bag.

Sabich

Sabich is a known vegetarian Israeli "street food" sandwich which is basically pita stuffed with fried eggplant and hard boiled eggs. This egg-free (or eggless) version is still flavorful and satisfying due to the rich combination of all the ingredients. These little sandwiches can totally be served for a breakfast or brunch party at your home, birthday or office. This recipe makes 8-10 small pitas

INGREDIENTS

1 eggplant, roasted

Tahini sauce

Israeli pickles, sliced

Some kalamata olives

1 jalapeno sliced (or harrisa spread)

Chopped Israeli salad

Some fresh parsley or cilantro

Some spring mix leaves

INSTRUCTIONS

1. Spread each pita with a 1-2 tbsp tahini sauce, place the 2 eggplant slices on top, add the pickles, olives and chopped salad, insert some parsley or cilantro, jalapeño and mixed greens and serve with some more pickles and tahini on the side. Enjoy.

COMFORT FOOD

Eggless Potato Kugel

This easy potato kugel is one of the signature dishes on my weekend menu. One of the reasons I love making it is because my kids enjoy it so much. For me, the best part is leftovers, of course, which go so amazingly with a simple, basic, fresh Israeli salad. Please note that because we are not using any eggs here, we must let this specific kugel cool for at least one hour before cutting into it. Otherwise it won't be firm enough. The best thing to do is to let it sit in the fridge for an hour or two and then the texture will be perfect. Once firmed, you can re-warm without any problem.

Eggless Potato Kugel

INGREDIENTS

1 cup raw green buckwheat soaked in water over night

2 big yellow onions, chopped and sautéed

1 onion, grated

8-10 yellow potatoes, peeled and grated

3 Tbsp grapeseed oil

1 tsp pink Himalayan salt (or more)

½ tsp black pepper (to taste)

INSTRUCTIONS

1. Preheat your oven to 350 F.
2. Start by sautéing 2 onions with a little grapeseed oil until golden.
3. Drain and wash the soaked buckwheat and place in a food processor along with 3 tbsp oil. Process for about 2 minutes until very very smooth! Transfer to a big bowl.
4. Grate the potatoes and 1 onion, (I use the same food processor) and transfer to the processed buckwheat bowl.
5. Add the sautéed onions, salt and pepper, making sure to taste if it needs additional salt and pepper. Mix well and transfer to a round or 9x13 baking pan lined with parchment paper.
6. Bake for one hour and 15 minutes. Remove from the oven to cool for at least one hour and enjoy!

Cauliflower “chicken balls” in Tomato Sauce

For me, comfort food is always something cooked in a rich sauce that can go with a bread or on a bed of rice to absorb the yummy flavors. These meatless patties are so filling and satisfying. They hold beautifully in the sauce. And here you have an extremely healthy dinner for the whole family!

Cauliflower "chicken balls" in Tomato Sauce

INGREDIENTS

For the sauce:

2 tbsp grapeseed oil

1 big onion, diced

2 garlic cloves, minced

1/2 cup fresh basil leaves

1 can 14.5 oz diced tomatoes

1/2 tsp turmeric

1 tsp paprika

1/2 tsp salt

1/4 tsp pepper

3 Tbsp tomato paste

2 1/2 cups water

For the 'chicken' balls:

1 cup raw buckwheat, soaked in water over night

1 head cauliflower, cleaned, washed and cooked until fork tender

2 medium onions, sautéed until golden

2 tbsp onion powder

1 tsp salt (more or less for your taste)

1/2 tsp pepper

2 tbsp chopped fresh parsley

1/2 cup quick 1 minutes oats (gf if needed)

INSTRUCTIONS

1. Strain and wash the buckwheat very well under running water. Transfer to a food processor and mix until you get a very smooth paste. Transfer to a bowl.
2. Drain and chop the cauliflower to small- medium chunks and add to the ground buckwheat bowl.
3. Sautee' the chopped onions until golden and add to the bowl. Add the spices, oats and parsley and mix with a wooden spoon until all the ingredients are well combined.
4. Fill a cup with hot water and an ice-cream scooper. Heat up a big wide nonstick skillet, add a few tbsp greapeseed oil.
5. Start by dipping your scooper into the hot water and then to the cauliflower mixture.

Carefully transfer to the hot skillet. Repeat this process until skillet has about 5-6 balls. Wait for about 2-3 minutes before you flip them. Once golden, flip, cook for 2 more minutes, and transfer to a plate lined with paper towels. Repeat this process until all the mixture is finished.

Now let's prepare the sauce:

6. In a wide pan sautee' the diced onion until translucent. Add the garlic,a few whole basil leaves and continue mixing for about a minute longer.
7. Add the diced tomatoes, tomato paste, water and spices. Mix and bring to a boil. Cover and simmer on very low for 20 minutes.
8. Add the cauliflower chicken balls, cover for 10 minutes and serve on a bed of basmati rice. Sprinkle some more basil leaves and enjoy.

Chinese Vegan Stir Fry with Broccoli Nuggets

Who could have thought that these nuggets can easily be made from nutritious ingredients that are so vital to our body and diet. In this recipe, I have combined broccoli so it gives a body to the nuggets. If you or your kids are not consuming enough broccoli this is a great way to incorporate it easily. (You can also try it with adding rice or 1 cup soaked TVP)

Chinese Vegan Stir Fry with Broccoli Nuggets

INGREDIENTS

1 1/2 cups green buckwheat, soaked overnight

1 head of broccoli, cleaned, washed

3 green onions, chopped

3 Tbsp tamari/soy sauce

1 tsp toasted sesame oil

1 tsp ginger powder

11/2 tsp garlic powder

3 Tbsp coconut sugar or your desired

sweetener

Dash of black pepper

For the stir fry:

3 green onions, chopped

4 garlic cloves, chopped

2 slices fresh ginger

1 red bell pepper

10 baby Portobello mushrooms

½ cup teriyaki sauce

2 tsp corn starch mixed with 1 cup water

Sesame seeds to garnish

INSTRUCTIONS

1. Bring a big pot of salted water to a boil and cook the broccoli florets for 6 minutes. Drain, let cool a bit and chop to small chunks.
2. Place the soaked buckwheat in a colander and wash under running water. Transfer to a food processor and mix well until smooth. Transfer to a bowl. Add the chopped green onions, chopped broccoli, soy, coconut sugar, oil, ginger and garlic powder to the mixture, mix with a spoon and check for flavors to your taste. (You may add more ginger, sweetener or soy).
3. Heat up a big wide nonstick skillet and spray some grapeseed oil. Use a small tsp and add the mixture as if you are shaping small drops of nuggets. Allow to form for a minute or so and flip with a fork. (These can burn easily so make sure the pan is not too hot, but in order

not to stick make sure the pan is not cold either). Repeat the process until mixture is done.

4. **Note: You may skip this step and bake those little nuggets in a preheated 400 degree oven for 15-18 minutes. (Place on a baking sheet lined with parchment paper and spray with a thin layer of oil)**

Now let's make the sauce:

Heat up a big wide nonstick skillet over medium-high heat. Add the garlic and ginger and mix constantly for 30 seconds. Add the pepper, and mushrooms and mix for 2 minutes. Add the teriyaki sauce mixed with water and corn starch. Finally, add the nuggets, mix and allow the sauce to thicken slightly. Garnish with green onions and serve on white basmati rice.

Corn Schnitzel

Regardless of being conscious about health or a plant-based diet, corn schnitzel was always a big part of my childhood menu. Once I became a mother and got exposed to a healthier diet, I learned that even vegan food, such as corn schnitzel can be extremely processed and really unhealthy, something I would not buy or give my kids. But something in me was always craving the unforgettable taste of the warm corn and the crispy crunchy bite of these store bought corn schnitzels. Also, I knew I wanted my kids to enjoy it too. So after many experiments, I have come to the conclusion that the recipe below is the closest in look and taste to the real deal. And just like the store bought ones, tofu is pretty much the base to these yummy schnitzels. So, I have decided to use it here as well. These delicious schnitzels are so filling, easy, impressive and kid friendly. They are gone fast! Great for school with some pasta and fresh veggies.

Corn Schnitzel

INGREDIENTS

2 ½ cups cooked brown rice

½ pack firm tofu (drained)

1 can organic corn (drained)

2-3 Tbsp flour of your choice (oat, white spelt, corn)

2 Tbsp soy sauce

2 Tbsp organic ketchup

1 tsp salt (approximately)

½ tsp pepper

Sautéed onion (optional)

For coating:

Panko breadcrumbs (gf if needed)

INSTRUCTIONS

1. Place the rice, tofu, and half of the corn amount in a food processor and pulse a few times.
2. Transfer to a bowl and add the flour, the rest of the unprocessed corn, and spices. Mix and place mixture in the fridge for 30 minutes.
3. Prepare a wide bowl or tray with breadcrumbs. Using wet hands form patties. Then dip into breadcrumbs.
4. Place patties on a baking sheet lined with parchment paper. Spray some oil, sprinkle some salt and bake on 350 for 35 minutes.

Enjoy!

Vegan Matzah Ball Soup

There is nothing more nostalgic for me than growing up eating comforting matza ball soup every Friday. But since eggs are no longer a part of my kitchen, I was really missing this soup in my Friday cooking routine, while preparing for Shabbat. But then, I discovered the beautiful combination of tofu and matza meal together which create the puffy and fluffy effect that we all love. Since the soup has no chicken in it, we have to make sure that we make the broth as flavorful as it can get. That is why I add fresh ginger and lots of fresh herbs. But feel free to put your own touches and make your favorite broth.

Vegan Matzah Ball Soup

INGREDIENTS

For the mazah balls:

200 grams firm tofu, pat dry!

1 ½ cups matza meal

200 ml boiling water

¼ cup grapeseed oil

½ tbsp pink Himalayan salt

1 tbsp hawaij spice (can be found on Amazon)

¼ cup chopped dill

¼ cup chopped parsley

For the soup:

2 tbsp grapeseed oil

2 carrots, cut into chunks

1 zucchini, cut into medium chunks

1 butternut squash, cut into medium chunks

1 potato, cut into medium chunks

1 onion, diced

½ red bell pepper, diced

5 black peppercorns

Salt to taste

2 bay leaves

1 bunch fresh dill, washed and cleaned

4 big slices fresh ginger

Salt to taste

INSTRUCTIONS

1. Place the onion, red bell pepper and ginger in a deep soup pot with 2 tbsp oil, sauté until translucent. Add the rest of the vegetables except the dill. Fill the pot ¾ of the way with cold water. Bring to a boil and cook for 45 minutes or so, add some fresh dill (without chopping so that you can easily take it out later) and continue cooking for 10-15 minutes more.
2. While bringing 8 cups water to a boil in a deep wide pot, place the tofu in a food processor and pulse for a minute, add the matzah meal and hot water. Continue processing until it is all incorporated. Transfer to a bowl, add the spices, fresh herbs, oil and mix with your hands.
3. While the soup is cooking, we are going to prepare the matzah balls. Start shaping the balls and gently place them in the boiling water. Lower the heat, cover the pot, and cook for 20

minutes until cooked through.

4. When the soup is ready, serve some veggies, lots of broth and 2-3 matzah balls.

NOTE: I always recommend doing a texture test before cooking all the mixture. Place 2-3 matzah balls in the boiling water. Cook on low for 15-20 minutes. If from some reason they fall apart, add to the uncooked mixture in the bowl 1 tbsp chickpea flour (or regular flour). They won't be as puffed but definitely hold the shape nicely!

Eggplant Schnitzel

Growing up in Israel and eating lots of eggplants is a natural thing. On weekdays, my Mom would slice an eggplant and dip it into some egg, and breadcrumbs. Then she would fry it with some oil and we all called it eggplant schnitzel. We would put it in a pita with hummus, tomato, hot pepper and enjoy it for lunch or a late breakfast. In the eggless world we have to find a way to replace the egg as a binder for the breadcrumbs to stick and get a nice crunchy coating.

In this picture I cut the eggplant lengthwise. But feel free to cut the eggplant into regular medium round slices. They are easier to handle and cook faster that way. You can totally bake it but the texture and color will be a bit different than the fried one. (If you choose to pan fry it, make sure it has a chance to cook through so its better to use medium heat.)

Eggplant Schnitzel

INGREDIENTS

1 eggplant, sliced

¼ cup white spelt flour (or chickpea flour, or regular flour)

¼ cup water

½ tsp cumin

½ tsp paprika

½ tsp salt

Pinch of black pepper

Panko or golden breadcrumbs

Oil for frying or for spraying

INSTRUCTIONS

1. Prepare the batter to replace the eggs by whisking together flour, water and spices. Set aside. Prepare a wide dish with 1 cup breadcrumbs and some salt.
2. Peel the eggplant and cut into your desired shape.
3. Dip the eggplant into the flour batter, coat very well, then transfer to the breadcrumbs dish and place on a plate.
4. If frying: Prepare a skillet with some shallow oil, heat to 350, and fry for at least 4 minutes on each side.
5. If baking: Preheat your oven to 425 F. Place the coated eggplants on a baking sheet lined with parchment paper. Spray some grapeseed oil and bake for 20-25 minutes until golden brown.
6. Place on a green salad with some fresh lemon squeezed. Or place in a pita or a baguette with some hummus and veggies.

Enjoy!

GF Falafel Kabob Platter

We all have those days where we crave something street-food and wished it was healthier. That is why I came up with this beautiful and satisfying pan seared and gluten free falafel-kabob platter. Surround it with tahini, amba (tangy mango pickle condiment), cabbage and Israeli salad. You can definitely go ahead and form traditional round balls. But because there is no bread involved in this meal we want it to be more like finger food that's easy to grab and dip. These kabobs are moist, fluffy due to my secret ingredient, the tahini. I added a couple of Tbsp into the falafel bowl and it made all the difference in the world. These can also be baked so make sure to spray some oil before baking. Or, just like in the picture here, you can shallow pan sear them with some grapeseed oil until golden brown on each side.

GF Falafel Kabob Platter

INGREDIENTS

2 cups dry chickpeas- must be soaked in water overnight (up to 24 hours with 1 tsp baking soda)

8 garlic cloves

1 big onion- peeled and cut into 4

2 big handfuls of fresh cilantro

1 handfuls parsley

½ jalapeno pepper (Or ½ red bell pepper, optional)

1 tsp baking soda

2 tbsp raw tahini

2 tsp ground cumin

1-2 tsp salt

Pepper

2 tbsp chickpea flour

2 tbsp olive oil

INSTRUCTIONS

1. Place the onions, garlic, cilantro, parsley and jalapeno in a food processor and pulse until finely chopped. Transfer to a bowl.
2. Wash the chickpeas very well and add them to the same food processor. Finely chop. It would be better to do a few small batches and transfer to the chopped herbs bowl.
3. Once everything is in the bowl, add tahini, oil, salt, pepper, cumin, and chickpea flour. Mix very well, cover and place in the fridge for 15-30 minutes. Check if you need more salt and cumin to taste and then add the baking soda! (Don't be afraid to have very dominant flavors. It's necessary in this case).
4. Prepare a bowl of water to dip your hands, and shape falafel kabobs or some regular small falafel balls. Carefully place on a baking sheet lined with parchment paper.
5. Heat up some shallow layer of grapeseed oil in a nonstick pan. Sear each side for about 3-4 minutes until nice and golden. Place on a plate with paper towel to absorb the oil.
6. Serve with many fresh condiments such as: red and green cabbage, Israeli salad, pickles, lots of tahini and whatever you love.

For baking:

Preheat your oven to 420F.

Spray some grapeseed oil and bake for 20-25 minutes. Once golden brown take out and let cool for at least 10 minutes. Sprinkle some salt if needed, and enjoy with some fresh salads and tahini on the side.

Baked Breaded Cauliflower Tempura Bites

Cauliflower is one of the most loveable vegetables in our household. I make sure to serve it to my kids on weekly basis. What is so beautiful about this vegetable is that it is so versatile and there are so many things that can be done with it. One of them, is this incredibly tasty recipe, which is usually fried, that pleases any age, event or crowd.

INGREDIENTS

1 head cauliflower, cut into florets

1 cup chickpea flour

2/3 cup water + 2 tbsp

½ tsp baking powder

½ tbsp garlic powder

½ tbsp onion powder

1 tsp pink Himalayan salt

¼ tsp black pepper

2 tbsp organic ketchup

1.5 cups panko breadcrumbs (GF if needed)

INSTRUCTIONS

1. Preheat oven to 375 F. on a roasting feature or 400 F. on regular bake.
2. Arrange a baking sheet lined with parchment paper.
3. Place chickpea flour in a bowl along with the spices and baking powder and mix. Add the water slowly, and whisk constantly until very smooth. Add the ketchup, and set aside.
4. Prepare a deep dish with bread crumbs.
5. Dip the florets into the chickpea batter, then transfer to the breadcrumbs and lay on the baking sheet.
6. Spray an even coating of oil over the cauliflower and bake for 35-40 minutes until cooked through and golden brown. (Every oven is different, so baking time may vary).

Lentil Loaf

Lentils are such a valuable factor in the vegan world as they are full of protein, and so versatile in so many dishes. I have seen so many lentil loaves falling apart on the table. I knew I had to try to change it so you can wow your thanksgiving table with this masterpiece. It was way easier than I thought. Firm, far from dry and with the perfect texture. My family couldn't stop eating it and I kept asking my kids who wants more "lentil cake". The red sauce is totally optional. You may try to top it with some gravy as well.

Lentil Loaf

INGREDIENTS

1 cup raw buckwheat, soaked overnight

¾-1 cup precooked lentils

1 big sweet potato, grated

2 big red onions, chopped

¾ cup toasted walnuts

2 tbsp toasted sesame seeds

3 tbsp tomato paste

1 tsp cumin

1 tsp thyme

½ tsp dry rosemary

¼ tsp cinnamon

½ tsp black pepper

1 tsp salt (or to your taste)

3 tbsp chopped parsley or cilantro

2 tbsp olive oil

For the red sauce:

1/3 cup ketchup

1-2 tbsp pure maple syrup

2 tbsp mustered

1 tbsp apple cider vinegar

1 tbsp balsamic vinegar

INSTRUCTIONS

1. Drain, wash and grind the soaked buckwheat in a food processor until very smooth. Add the cooked lentils and pulse for 2 seconds just until almost smooth. Transfer to a bowl.
2. Place 2 tbsp oil in a skillet and sauté the onions for 2-3 minutes. Add the grated sweet potato and cook until soft. About 7 minutes.
3. Meanwhile toast the nuts and sesame seeds in the oven or in a dry skillet just until golden. Transfer to a food processor and chop into little crumbs. (not too small)
4. Preheat your oven to 350 F.
5. In a big bowl combine ground buckwheat and lentils, chopped nuts, cooked onions and sweet potatoes, spices, herbs. Mix well and adjust seasonings.
6. Place in a loaf pan lined with parchment paper. Flatten the top with a wet spatula.
7. Bake in the oven for 45 minutes. You may chose to glaze it while its still baking, 10 minutes before its ready, or once you are serving it (which is the way I prefer).
8. For the glaze red sauce: combine all ingredients in a small sauce pan and cook on low for 3-5 minutes.

Buckwheat Garden Arugula Pizza

Eating healthy was NEVER so easy, UNTIL NOW! I can't stress enough how blessed and excited I feel to share this revolutionary recipe with you and change your life forever! You'll never think that "junk food" can be made so healthily, with the right flavor and TEXTURE. No need for a cauliflower crust loaded with eggs and cheese! This gluten-free pizza is so easy to prepare and it is totally going to be on your weekly menu. Feed your family and kids with zero guilt and show the world that buckwheat pizza is the new way to enjoy "junk-food" happily and healthily.

Buckwheat Garden Arugula Pizza

INGREDIENTS

For the crust:

1 cup raw buckwheat, soaked over night

½ cup almond flour

½ cup water

1 tsp dry yeast

2 tbsp olive oil

1 tsp salt

For the sauce:

400 grams diced canned tomatoes

1 can tomato paste (6 oz)

2 tbsp olive oil

1 tbsp red wine vinegar

1 tsp salt

1 tbsp black pepper

1.5 tbsp dry oregano

Pinch of brown sugar

INSTRUCTIONS

1. Preheat your oven to 350 F.
2. Prepare a round pizza tray lined with parchment paper.
3. Drain, wash and grind the soaked buckwheat in a food processor until very smooth.
4. To the food processor bowl add the water, almond flour, yeasts, olive oil, salt and mix very well. You'll get a smooth runny consistency.
5. Leave covered and let sit for 10 minutes.
6. Lightly oil the parchment paper. Pour the mixture and spread evenly (make sure its not too too thin). Bake at 350 for 20 minutes. (poke with a fork after 10 minutes to allow air to escape from the bottom)
7. Prepare the sauce by placing all the ingredients in a food processor. Blend until very smooth.
8. Take out the pizza crust from the oven, pour as much as you desire from the sauce, top with your favorite toppings. Place back in the oven and raise the temperature to 385 F. (freeze the rest of the sauce for next time)

9. Bake for 15-25 minutes more.

Favorite toppings:

Drained chickpeas
Kalamata olives
Onions
Tomatoes
Fresh arugula
Jalapeno pepper

Nostalgic Spinach Quiche

There is something magical about quiches that I can't explain. I absolutely love this light and elegant food on my plate served with a fresh green leafy salad. But we all know what it takes to get the right texture when not using eggs. Adding plenty of flour, breadcrumbs, oil, and the consistency is just not right. We end up defeating the whole purpose of keeping this dish healthy. But luckily not anymore! This revolutionary recipe is just about to change your life forever. It gets as good as it can get. Not compromising on texture, flavor and health. This one gets even better the next day. And feel free to combine it with some Swiss chard if you'd like.

INGREDIENTS

1 cup raw green buckwheat, soaked overnight

½ a box baby spinach, roughly chopped (1/2 pound total)

3 red onions, chopped

½ cup almond flour

2 tbsp grapeseed or olive oil

1 tsp baking powder (Aluminum free)

1/3 cup unsweetened plant milk (or water)

Salt and paper to taste

INSTRUCTIONS

1. Heat up a wide skillet with 1-2 tbsp olive oil. Chop and sauté the onions until golden brown. Add the chopped spinach and season nicely with salt and pepper. Mix and cook for 3-5 minutes until soft and wilted. Allow to cool.
2. Preheat your oven to 350 F.
3. Drain, wash the soaked buckwheat, place in a food processor and run until very very smooth. Once completely smooth add the water/ milk, almond flour (or soaked cashews), oil and run until all incorporated.
4. Pour the buckwheat mixture into the sautéed spinach mixture and combine very well. Season some more with some salt and pepper and add a touch of nutmeg if you'd like.
5. Transfer to a round deep cake pan which was lined with parchment paper, sprayed with a touch of oil.
6. Bake for 45-60 minutes unit firm.   Let cool for 20-30 minutes before slicing.

BREAKFAST

Apple Cinnamon Pancakes

These pancakes are amazing for breakfast or brunch! Very filling and yet you still feel light and refreshed. Very easy to make, using only a few ingredients and you have an easy & nutritious meal to start the day.

INGREDIENTS

1 cup raw buckwheat, soaked in water over night

1 cup almond milk (or any plant milk)

1/2 cup quick 1-minute oats (GF if needed)

1 tsp baking powder

1 sweet apple, peeled and grated

1 tsp cinnamon

2 Tbsp brown sugar or maple syrup

¼ cup toasted pecans, finely chopped (optional)

INSTRUCTIONS

1. Soak 1 cups raw, untoasted green buckwheat (175g) in water for 6 hours, or overnight. Transfer to a colander and wash with lots of water until water is running very clear. This process could take few minutes.
2. Place the buckwheat in a blender and add EXACTLY 1 1/4 cups milk+ 1/2 a cup quick 1- minute oats and turn the blender on for 2-3 minutes until very smooth!
3. Transfer the mixture to a bowl; add the grated apple, sugar, baking powder, cinnamon, pecans and mix.
4. Heat up a wide NONSTICK SKILLET and spray a thin coat of coconut or grapeseed oil. Pan must be hot.
5. Start placing 1/3 or 1/2 cup of the batter (depending on the size you prefer) on the skillet. Wait for bubbles and for some color. Flip and wait about 2-3 minute (you may lower the heat to medium and cover the pancakes while they cook) and transfer to a plate. Repeat this process until everything is done.
6. Drizzle with pure maple syrup and enjoy!

Zucchini Pancakes

These amazing pancakes are light and moist with a soft delicate texture. They can go so nicely next to a fresh green salad for a light breakfast or brunch.

INGREDIENTS

1 cup raw buckwheat, soaked in water overnight

1 1/4cup water

1 onion, chopped

1 tbsp olive oil

3-4 medium zucchini, grated

1 cup quick oats

¼ tsp baking powder

1 tbsp onion powder

3 tbsp chopped parsley or dill

1 tsp salt (or more)

1/2 tsp pepper

1-2 tbsp grapeseed oil (or spray)

INSTRUCTIONS

1. Sautee' chopped onion in 1 tbsp oil until nice and golden. Meanwhile, drain the soaked buckwheat and wash very well under running water. Transfer to a food processor and blend well until very smooth. Transfer to a bowl.
2. To the bowl: Add grated zucchini, sautéed onions, salt, pepper, onion powder, baking powder, chopped parsley/dill, oats and water. Mix.
3. Heat up a big wide nonstick skillet, add1 tbsp grapeseed oil.
4. Scoop 1/3 or ½ a cup of the mixture and transfer carefully to the hot skillet. Repeat to fill the skillet with about 2-3 pancakes. Wait about 2-3 minutes. Once golden and firm on the bottom, flip, cook for 2-3 more minutes and transfer to a plate lined with paper towels. Repeat this process until all the mixture is finished.

Buckwheat Tortillas

There is nothing like eating real laffa, warm fresh pita, or flat bread! But what do you do when you can not consume too much of it, or in many cases any of it?! This amazing recipe is one of the best things you can add to your diet. It will literally change your life. Buckwheat is full of iron. It fills you up and its one of the best super foods nature offers. The great thing about this recipe is that it's gluten free, oil free, dairy free and you can eat it with almost anything that comes to your mind. The flavor is very mild and the texture is nice and soft.

Whenever we cook with buckwheat we must use a NONSTICK SKILLET. The first tortilla might not come out the best, (like the first batch of pancakes, they almost never come out right). Just make sure the skillet is really hot and don't flip before it's ready on the first side.

Buckwheat Tortillas

INGREDIENTS

2 cups raw buckwheat

1/2 cup quick 1-minute oats (gf if needed)

Pinch of salt

2 1/2 cups water

INSTRUCTIONS

1. Soak 2 cups raw, untoasted green buckwheat (350g) in water for 6 hours, or overnight.
2. Transfer to a colander and wash with lots of water until water is running very clear. This process could take few minutes.
3. Place the buckwheat and oats in a blender and add EXACTLY 2 1/2 cups water. Add a pinch of salt and turn the blender on for 2-3 minutes until very smooth!
4. Heat up a wide NONSTICK SKILLET and start placing 1/3 or 1/2 cup of the batter (depending on the size you prefer) on the skillet. With a ladle, work in a circular motion to spread it on the skillet quickly, as if you are evenly spreading a pizza sauce. Wait for bubbles and for some color. Once the edges are dry, flip, wait a minute, then transfer to a plate. Repeat this process until everything is done.
5. Now fill it with whatever you wish.
6. Some suggestions are mashed avocado, diced tomatoes, sliced jalapeno, chickpeas and cilantro. I suggest sprinkle of salt and a touch of some good olive oil. If you wish to roll it, just use slightly less condiments and spread it as flat as you can.

Oat Scramble

Who said that oats should only be served sweet?! Oats are one of the healthiest grains on earth! I personally would always prefer a savory dish over a sweet one. This wholesome breakfast will change the way you eat and look at oats. This grain is so versatile and nourishing. So whenever you crave some scrambled eggs, try this dish first.

Oat Scramble

INGREDIENTS

8 baby Portobello mushrooms, sliced

½ onion, diced

½ a tomato, diced

3 tbsp chopped cilantro

1/2 tbsp grapeseed oil

1/2 cup whole oatmeal (old fashion oats)

1/4 cup 1 minute quick oats (or oat flour)

1/2 teaspoon of turmeric powder

salt and pepper to taste

1/3-1/2 cup water

INSTRUCTIONS

1. Heat up 1 tbsp oil over medium high heat. Add the onions and mushrooms and stir occasionally for about 5 minutes.
2. Add salt, pepper and turmeric and mix for 30 seconds or so. Add the diced tomato, stir until melted down.
3. Add the 2 types of oats along with the water. Mix and cover. Cook on the lowest heat for about 6-9 minutes until al dente. (soft but not mushy) Add water if needed. Sprinkle some cilantro or dill.
4. Serve with sliced avocado and fresh vegetables.

Note: If desired, add some dry chili flakes or sriracha sauce on top.

Tofu Scramble

It took me such a long time to adopt tofu into my diet. It was hard for me to get used to the texture and flavor that was many times overpowering the flavors I was hoping to get. But... I never stopped trying! I kept experimenting with this versatile product until I finally got it right! This dish is by far my kid's favorite breakfast. It is rich and filling and so so flavorful.

INGREDIENTS

1 Package Organic Firm or Extra Firm Tofu

1.5 tbsp oil (I use grapeseed)

2 onions, chopped

1 garlic clove, minced (or 1 tsp powder)

½-1 tsp turmeric powder

Salt and pepper to taste

½ tsp Indian black salt (optional)

INSTRUCTIONS

1. Pat dry the tofu and with your hands and break into big crumbs. Place on a clean paper towel and set aside.
2. Heat up a nonstick pan with oil and add the chopped onions. Sautee for about 5 minutes until starting to get golden. Add the garlic and mix for another 30 seconds or so.
3. Add the tofu and sprinkle the turmeric evenly. Mix constantly until all the crumbs are yellow coated. Generously sprinkle salt and pepper and continue mixing for about 2-3 minutes until the tofu is nice and golden.
4. Serve with a fresh salad or sliced vegetables, bread, avocado, olives and enjoy breakfast with your loved ones.

Eggless French Toast

Although I would almost always prefer savory foods over sweet ones, I find it really hard to resist the smell and taste of this nostalgic childhood treat made from our Shabbat Challah leftovers. This recipe takes me all the way to the place where comfort food is called- home. It is now possible to have it eggless, and it is no less than perfection!

INGREDIENTS

8-12 slices bread (brioche, challah)

2 cup plant based vanilla milk

3 tbsp maple syrup

3 tbsp corn starch

1.5 tbsp nutritional yeasts

Pinch of salt

½ tsp cinnamon

2 tbsp coconut oil

INSTRUCTIONS

1. Place the corn starch in a mixing bowl and add 3 tbsp of the milk. Whisk very well until there are no any clumps. Add the rest of the milk, and the rest of the ingredients and mix.
2. Heat up a nonstick skillet over medium heat and add a little coconut oil. Dip the bread into the batter for about 2 seconds on each side and place in the pan. About 2-3 in a batch, depending on the size of your skillet.
3. Repeat until everything is nice and golden. Serve with some pure maple syrup and fresh berries and enjoy while its hot.

Enjoy!

HEALTHY TREATS

Vegan Brownie Fudge Cake

If you ask me at any given time what would I pick, a cake or a pita with an eggplant, jalapeño, cilantro and tahini I would most likely pick the pita. I was blessed not to have a sweet tooth. I love savory spicy food too much. BUT, when it comes to brownies…I really can't say no. There is something comforting about the chewy texture of brownies! Something that is a little hard to mimic when no longer using eggs. These Gluten-free brownies are moist, chocolaty, chewy and absolutely yummy.

Vegan Brownie Fudge Cake

INGREDIENTS

1/3 cup raw green buckwheat, soaked overnight

1 tbsp Grapeseed Or coconut oil

1/2 cup coconut sugar

1/4 cup soy milk

3/4 cups almond flour

1 tsp baking powder

1/3 cup cocoa powder

Some sliced almonds (optional)

¼-1/2 cup chocolate chips

INSTRUCTIONS

1. Preheat your oven to 350 F.
2. Strain and rinse buckwheat very well under water. Place in a food processor and blend until very smooth. To the processed buckwheat add the oil, soy milk, sugar, cocoa powder and mix. Set aside.
3. In another bowl sift the almond flour and mix with baking powder. Add the chocolate chips and mix.
4. Combine the wet ingredients with the dry. Add some sliced almonds, fold gently until well incorporated.
5. Using a WET spatula transfer the batter to a prepared brownie baking sheet lined with parchment paper. Pressing and tighten the batter towards the corners. Once you've got an even layer, place in the oven and bake for 18-22 minutes. It might still feel very soft once taken out. Allow it to sit for at least 30 minutes or preferably overnight in the fridge.

Tahini Cookies/Muffins

These oil free cookies are my kid's favorite. Soft, airy, chocolaty and full of nutritious. I love sending them to school as they hold their shape nicely. For freshness, best kept in the fridge.

INGREDIENTS

1 cup raw green buckwheat, soaked over night

½ cup almond flour

1.5 tsp baking soda

1.5 tsp baking powder

1/4 cup raw tahini

1/3- 1/2 cup maple syrup/honey

1 tsp cinnamon

1/3 cup chocolate chips

INSTRUCTIONS

1. Preheat your oven to 350 F.
2. Drain, wash and grind the soaked buckwheat in a food processor until very smooth. Transfer to a bowl.
3. Add almond flour, baking soda, baking powder, tahini paste, chocolate chips, cinnamon, and mix well.
4. Using a wet spoon or an ice-cream scooper, scoop from the batter and place on a baking sheet lined with parchment paper.
5. Bake on 350 for 12 minutes. Take out and let cool completely.
6. For freshness, best store in the fridge. You may rewarm in the microwave for 10 seconds.

Orange Muffins

Not that I'm a big fan of cakes and sweet food in general, but I too, grew up eating the nostalgic yellow sponge cake, full of flavor, aroma and comfort. There are many vegan cakes these days, however, I have not yet came across a simple yellow cake that comes out soft, wet and not falling apart. These orange muffins are the answer to the vegan cake that can serve as a base for your child's birthday cake or muffins for your weekend breakfast cravings! You can bake this batter in an English loaf pan or double quantities if you want to freeze and warm up later.

Orange Muffins

INGREDIENTS

1.5 cups white spelt flour (or regular white flour)

¾-1 cup organic cane sugar

1 tsp baking soda

1 tbsp orange zest (A must)

½ cup freshly squeezed orange juice

½ cup soy milk (or water/ plant milk)

1/3 cup grapessed oil

1 tsp vanilla extract

1 tbsp apple cider vinegar

INSTRUCTIONS

1. Preheat oven to 350 F.
2. Combine dry ingredients in a big bowl: flour, baking soda, sugar and mix.
3. Combine wet ingredients in another bowl: juice, milk, oil, vanilla, orange zest and vinegar. Mix.
4. Slowly pour wet into the dry until all incorporated. Be careful not to over mix.
5. Transfer to a pan or muffin tin and bake for 20-25 minutes, or until knife or toothpick comes out dry and clean.

Enjoy!

Peanut Butter Cookies

These delicate cookies are the perfect answer to your peanut butter and chocolate cravings. Gluten free, oil free, easy to prepare, and so amazing with a warm cup of coffee or tea.

INGREDIENTS

1 cup raw green buckwheat, soaked over night

½ cup almond flour

1.5 tsp baking soda

1.5 tsp baking powder

1/3 cup natural peanut butter

1/3 cup maple syrup/honey

1/3 cup chocolate chips

Small pinch of salt (optional)

INSTRUCTIONS

1. Preheat your oven to 350 F.
2. Drain, wash and grind the soaked buckwheat in a food processor until very smooth. Transfer to a bowl.
3. Add almond flour, baking soda, baking powder, peanut butter, and chocolate chips and mix well.
4. Using a wet spoon or an ice-cream scooper, scoop batter and drop on a baking sheet lined with parchment paper.
5. Bake on 350 for 12 minutes. Take out and let cool completely.
6. For freshness store in the fridge. You may rewarm in the microwave for 10 seconds or so.

Sweet Potato Cookies

Sweet potatoes are one of the healthiest carbs to consume in the morning due to their low glycolic index. Whenever I can, I try to incorporate them in my dishes so my little kids can enjoy the health benefit that this amazing vegetable offers. This recipe gets even healthier because of the anti-inflammatory spices that it contains. Perfect on the go, kid friendly and absolutely delicious.

INGREDIENTS

1 cup raw green buckwheat, soaked over night

3/4 cup almond flour

1.5 tsp baking soda

1.5 tsp baking powder

1/2 cup mashed sweet potato

2 tbsp grapeseed oil

1/3 cup maple syrup

1 tsp cinnamon

1 tsp pumpkin spice

1/3 cup chocolate chips or chunks

INSTRUCTIONS

1. Preheat your oven to 350 F.
2. Place 1 small diced sweet potato in a small bowl with 3 tbsp water and cook in the microwave for 6-8 minutes. Take out, remove the water and skin, mash well with a fork.
3. Drain, wash and grind the soaked buckwheat in a food processor until very smooth. Transfer to a bowl.
4. Add almond flour, baking soda, baking powder, ½ cup sweet potato, oil, chocolate chunks, and spices. Mix well.
5. Using a wet spoon or an ice-cream scooper, scoop from the batter and place on a baking sheet lined with parchment paper.
6. Bake at 350 for 12-15 minutes. Take out and let cool completely.
7. For freshness, best stored in the fridge. You may rewarm in the microwave for 10 seconds.

Baked Mini Banana Pancakes/ Muffins

As a mother of 4 year old twin toddlers and a two year old daughter, I always think about snacks that I can carry around wherever I go. Breakfast on the go is always a priority, and these soft little treats are just perfect every time.

INGREDIENTS

1 cup raw green buckwheat, soaked over night

3/4th cup almond flour

1.5 tsp baking soda

1.5 tsp baking powder

3 ripe bananas, mashed

2 tbsp coconut or grapeseed oil

1/4 cup maple syrup/honey

1 tsp vanilla extract

1/3 cup chocolate chips

For muffins: Add ¾ cup water or plant-based milk to the batter. Bake for 20-22 minutes.

INSTRUCTIONS

1. Preheat your oven to 350 F.
2. Drain, wash and blend the soaked buckwheat in a food processor until very smooth. Transfer to a bowl.
3. Add almond flour, mashed bananas, baking soda, baking powder, chocolate chips, vanilla, and mix well.
4. Using a wet spoon or an ice-cream scooper, scoop from the batter and place on a baking sheet lined with parchment paper.
5. Bake at 350 F. for 12 minutes. Take out and let cool completely.
6. For freshness, best to store in the fridge. You may rewarm in the microwave for 10 seconds

Disclaimer !

Dear Readers,

It is important to note that food can be a sensitive matter to many. We all were raised in varied cultural backgrounds.

In time, life leads us to different places and stages. Some things we plan today, might not be what we choose to do in a year, 5 years, or 20 years from now, especially when we plan and prepare our menus.

I have a huge passion for cooking. I love food; I live and dream food all the time! Although this is a 100% vegan cookbook I'm NOT 100% fully Vegan. Ninety percent of the time I live a vibrant lifestyle of wholesome plant-based foods. But at times, I do allow myself and kids to eat non-vegan food. I do my best to choose better product qualities; but I strive for home-cooked meals that are plant-based rich, wholesome and healthy. I've learned through my journey not to judge anyone for their food choices. Instead I've chosen to educate, inspire, and never stop growing by learning about the gifts we find in natural unprocessed foods.

I don't like to label my food passion. I'm a human being and I have learned to listen to my body. The life choices my book presents which my own family follows, gives you living proof that the plant based diet can be rich, tasty, elegant, and nutritious. It is far from boring. I invite you now to try it for yourself!

With lots of respect,

Bat-El